As you begin to pay attention to your own

stories and what they say about you, you

will enter into the exciting process of becoming,

as you should be, the author of your own

life, the creator of your own possibilities.

MANDY AFTEL

ACKNOWLEDGEMENTS

WITH SPECIAL THANKS TO:

Jason Aldrich, Gloria Austin, Gerry Baird, Jay Baird, Neil Beaton, Josie Bissett, Laura Boro, Jim and Alyssa Darragh & Family, Jennifer and Matt Ellison & Family, Rob Estes, Michael and Leianne Flynn & Family, Sarah Forster, Jennifer Hurwitz, Heidi Jones, Carol Anne Kennedy, June Martin, Jessica Phoenix and Tom DesLongchamp, Janet Potter & Family, Diane Roger, Kirsten and Garrett Sessions, Kristel Wills, Clarie Yam and Erik Lee, Heidi Yamada & Family, Justi and Tote Yamada & Family, Bob and Val Yamada, Kaz and Kristin Yamada & Family, Tai and Joy Yamada, Anne Zadra, August and Arline Zadra, Dan Zadra, and Gus and Rosie Zadra.

CREDITS

Compiled by Kobi Yamada

Designed by Steve Potter

ISBN: 978-1-888387-58-2

6th Printing. 7500 09 08   Printed in China

EXPLORE every day.

COMPENDIUM™
INCORPORATED

live inspired.

Blessed are the
curious for they
shall have
adventures.

LOVELLE DRACHMAN

EXPLORE every day.

As you grow older,
you'll find that
the only things
you regret are
the things you
didn't do.

ZACHARY SCOTT

EXPLORE every day.

Do not be too timid
and squeamish about
your actions. All life
is an experiment.

RALPH WALDO EMERSON

EXPLORE every day.

...the first step...
shall be to lose
the way.

GALWAY KINNELL

EXPLORE every day.

Every one of
us has in him
a continent of
undiscovered
character.

EXPLORE every day.

To travel hopefully
is a better thing
than to arrive.

ROBERT LOUIS STEVENSON

EXPLORE every day.

I expand and
live in the warm
day like corn
and melons.

RALPH WALDO EMERSON

EXPLORE every day.

...if you are wise
and know the art of
travel, let yourself
go on the stream of
the unknown and
accept whatever
comes in the spirit
in which the gods
may offer it.

FREYA STARK

EXPLORE every day.

Travel is as much
a passion as
ambition or love.

LETITIA ELIZABETH

EXPLORE every day.

Any place that
we love becomes
our world.

UNKNOWN

EXPLORE every day.

Every step of
the journey is
the journey.

ZEN SAYING

EXPLORE every day.

The trail is the
thing, not the end
of the trail. Travel
too fast and you
miss all you are
traveling for.

LOUIS L'AMOUR

Never lose an
opportunity of
seeing anything
that is beautiful...

RALPH WALDO EMERSON

EXPLORE every day.

You can fall in
love at first sight
with a place as
well as a person.

ALEC WAUGH

EXPLORE every day.

As long as
habit and routine
dictate the pattern
of living, new
dimensions of
the soul will
not emerge.

HENRY VAN DYKE

EXPLORE every day.

The aim of life
is to live, and to
live means to be
aware, joyously,
drunkenly, serenely,
divinely aware.

HENRY MILLER

EXPLORE every day.

Some experiences
simply do not
translate. You have
to *go* to *know*.

KOBI YAMADA

EXPLORE every day.

Seek and you will
find. Don't be
willing to accept
an ordinary life.

SALLE MERRILL REDFIELD

EXPLORE every day.

Life is always best
on the open road.

OLIVER JONES

EXPLORE every day.

One doesn't
discover new
lands without
consenting to
lose sight of
the shore...

ANDRÉ GIDE

EXPLORE every day.

Discoveries are
often made by
not following
instructions, by
going off the
main road, by
trying the untried.

FRANK TYGER

EXPLORE every day.

The purpose of
education is to
replace an empty
mind with an
open one.

MALCOLM FORBES

EXPLORE every day.

People travel
to wonder at
the height of
the mountains,
at the huge waves
of the sea, at the
long course of
rivers...and they
pass by themselves
without wondering.

ST. AUGUSTINE

EXPLORE every day.

All growth is a
leap in the dark,
a spontaneous
unpremeditated
act without benefit
of experience.

HENRY MILLER

EXPLORE every day.

Wake up and live.

BOB MARLEY

EXPLORE every day.

The less of routine
the more of life.

AMOS BRONSON ALCOTT

EXPLORE every day.

Life, we learn too
late, is in the living,
the tissue of every
day and hour.

STEPHEN LEACOCK

EXPLORE every day.

...oh for a life of
sensations rather
than of thoughts!

JOHN KEATS

EXPLORE every day.

The man who views
the world at 50
the same as he
did at 20 has
wasted 30 years
of his life.

MUHAMMAD ALI

EXPLORE every day.

I began to have
an idea of my
life, not as the
slow shaping of
achievement to fit
my preconceived
purposes, but
as the gradual
discovery and
growth of a
purpose which
I did not know.

JOANNA FIELD

No journey is too
great if you find
what you seek.

UNKNOWN

EXPLORE every day.

We find what we
search for—or,
if we don't find it,
we become it.

JESSAMYN WEST

EXPLORE every day.

Imagination is
a poor substitute
for experience.

HAVELOCK ELLIS

EXPLORE every day.

It is only in adventure
that some people
succeed in knowing
themselves—in
finding themselves.

ANDRÉ GIDE

EXPLORE every day.

Traveling...is
either and escape
or a discovery.

ROSIE THOMAS

EXPLORE every day.

Visit the home
of your ancestors.
Walk the hills or
villages where they
were born. Feel
their dreams, hopes
and aspirations.

DAN ZADRA

EXPLORE every day.

A frontier is never
a place; it is a
time and a way
of life.

HAL BORLAND

EXPLORE every day.

Is not this the true
romantic feeling—
not to desire to
escape life, but to
prevent life from
escaping you?

THOMAS WOLFE

The main thing is
that we hear and
enjoy life's music
everywhere.

THEODORE FONTANE

EXPLORE every day.

Live out your
dreams and
fantasies....sit
for hours at
sidewalk cafes
and drink with
your heroes.
Make pilgrimages
to Mougins
and Abiquiu.

FRITZ SHOULDER

EXPLORE every day.

My favorite thing
is to go where
I've never been.

DIANE ARBUS

EXPLORE every day.

Laughter has no
foreign accent.

PAUL LOWNEY

EXPLORE every day.

The fool wonders,
the wise man travels.

THOMAS FULLER

EXPLORE every day.

Nobody can
experience our
lives for us.

CHARLOTTE JOKO BECK

EXPLORE every day.

Life is uncharted
territory. It reveals
its story one
moment at a time.

LEO BUSCAGLIA

EXPLORE every day.

Breathe in
experience....

MURIEL RUKEYSER

EXPLORE every day.

Spend the
afternoon;
you can't take
it with you.

ANNIE DILLARD

EXPLORE every day.

We live in a
wonderful world
full of beauty,
charm and
adventure. There
is no end to the
adventures that we
can have if only
we seek them with
our eyes open.

JAWAHARLAL NEHRU

EXPLORE every day.

Where is the organ
of wonder situated?
Immediately above
ideality. What is
its function? To
inspire a love of the
strange and new.

UNKNOWN

EXPLORE every day.

Life is not
a problem to
be solved,
but a mystery
to be lived.

THOMAS MERTON

EXPLORE every day.

Not all those who
wander are lost.

J.R.R. TOLKIEN

Without
experience there
is little wisdom.

APOCRYPHA

EXPLORE every day.

Certainly, travel
is more than the
seeing of sights;
it is a change that
goes on, deep and
permanent, in the
ideas of living.

MIRIAM BEARD

EXPLORE every day.

When you
travel, your first
discovery is that
you do not exist.

ELIZABETH HARDWICK

EXPLORE every day.

I am never happier
than when I am
alone in a foreign
city; it is as if
I had become
invisible.

STORM JAMESON

EXPLORE every day.

This is what
travel is about.
We strain to renew
our capacity for
wonder, to shock
ourselves into
astonishment
once again.

SHANA ALEXANDER

EXPLORE every day.

To awaken quite
alone in a strange
town is one of
the pleasantest
sensations in
the world.

FREYA STARK

EXPLORE every day.

We travel, some of
us forever, to seek
other states, other
lives, other souls.

ANAÏS NIN

EXPLORE every day.

I have learned this
strange thing, too,
about travel: one
may return to a
place and, quite
unexpectedly,
meet oneself still
lingering there
from the last time.

HELEN BEVINGTON

EXPLORE every day.

The true fruit of
travel is perhaps
the feeling of
being nearly
everywhere
at home.

FREYA STARK

EXPLORE every day.

The place you
have left forever
is always there
for you to see
whenever you
shut your eyes.

JAN MYRDAL

EXPLORE every day.

Trips don't end
when we return
home—in a sense
it's when they
usually begin.

AGNES E. BENEDICT

EXPLORE every day.

If one considered
life as a simple
loan, one would
perhaps be
less exacting.
We possess
actually nothing;
everything goes
through us.

EUGÈNE DELACROIX

As you walk and
eat and travel,
be where you are.
Otherwise you
will miss most
of your life.

BUDDHA

EXPLORE every day.

Food is our
common ground,
a universal
experience.

JAMES BEARD

EXPLORE every day.

I never eat when
I can dine.

MAURICE CHEVALIER

EXPLORE every day.

While you are
upon the earth,
enjoy the good
things that
are here....

JOHN SELDEN

EXPLORE every day.

Every now and
then go away
and have a little
relaxation...to
remain constantly
at work will
diminish your
judgment.

LEONARDO DA VINCI

EXPLORE every day.

English sign seen
in a Paris elevator:
Please leave your
values at the
front desk.

UNKNOWN

EXPLORE every day.

I love to explore
and taste and
imagine.

OLIVER SACKS

EXPLORE every day.

I can't give you
a recipe to live
long—life is how
you live, how
you sleep, how
you eat, how you
drink, how you
work—life is
what you are.

DORA ZINA

EXPLORE every day.

I see nothing in
space as promising
as the view from
a Ferris wheel.

E.B. WHITE

EXPLORE every day.

Guard well your spare
moments. They are
like uncut diamonds.
Discard them and their
value will never be
known. Improve them
and they will become
the brightest gems in
a useful life.

RALPH WALDO EMERSON

EXPLORE every day.

When the days are
too short, chances
are you are living
at your best.

EARL NIGHTINGALE

You have to
take time to live.
Living takes time.

ELEANOR McMILLEN BROWN

EXPLORE every day.

Everywhere I go,
I find a poet
has been there
before me.

SIGMUND FREUD

EXPLORE every day.

If the Earth were
only a few feet in
diameter, floating
a few feet above a
field somewhere,
people would come
from everywhere
to marvel at it....

JOE MILLER

EXPLORE every day.

Take the
gentle path.

GEORGE HERBERT

EXPLORE every day.

All the way
to heaven is heaven.

ST. CATHERINE OF SIENA

EXPLORE every day.

Love has a way
of making places
sacred and
moments
meaningful.

JANET HOBSON

EXPLORE every day.

Live in each season
as it passes; breathe
the air, drink the
drink, taste the fruit...

HENRY DAVID THOREAU

EXPLORE every day.

I have just dropped
into the very place
I have been seeking,
but in everything
it exceeds all
my dreams.

ISABELLA BIRD

EXPLORE every day.

I think wherever
your journey takes
you, there are
new gods waiting
there, with divine
patience—and
laughter.

SUSAN M. WATKINS

EXPLORE every day.

He who would
travel happily
must travel light.

ANTOINE DE SAINT-EXUPÉRY

EXPLORE every day.

It is good to
collect things,
but it is better
to go on walks.

ANATOLE FRANCE

EXPLORE every day.

Practice seeing
things from
perspectives other
than your own.

STEPHANIE GILBERT

EXPLORE every day.

We are all travelers
in the wilderness of
this world...and the
best that we find in
our travels is an
honest friend.

ROBERT LOUIS STEVENSON

EXPLORE every day.

Anything,
everything, little
or big becomes
an adventure when
the right person
shares it.

KATHLEEN NORRIS

EXPLORE every day.

I look upon
every day to be
lost, in which I do
not make a new
acquaintance.

SAMUEL JOHNSON

EXPLORE every day.

Fear makes
strangers out
of people who
should be friends.

SHIRLEY MACLAINE

EXPLORE every day.

Help! I'm being
held "prisoner"
by my heredity
and environment.

DENNIS ALLEN

EXPLORE every day.

Once in a while
it really hits people
that they don't
have to experience
the world in the
way they have
been told to.

ALAN KEIGHTLEY

EXPLORE every day.

What is life if,
full of care, we
have no time to
sit and stare?

W. H. DAVIES

EXPLORE every day.

Life never becomes
a habit to me. It's
always a marvel.

KATHERINE MANSFIELD

EXPLORE every day.

Everything I learn
makes me see how
much more there is
to know and how
little time there
is in a lifetime
to learn it all.

TOM BROWN, JR.

EXPLORE every day.

Twenty years from
now you will be
more disappointed
by the things you
didn't do than by
the ones you did
do. So throw off
the bowlines, sail
away from the safe
harbor. Catch the
tradewinds in your
sails. Explore.
Dream. Discover.

MARK TWAIN

EXPLORE every day.

Lost, yesterday,
somewhere
between sunrise
and sunset, two
golden hours,
each set with sixty
diamond minutes.
No reward offered,
for they are gone
forever.

HORACE MANN

EXPLORE every day.

Before me lies the
edge of the world.
I am on my way
there running.

FROM A PAPAGO SONG

EXPLORE every day.

You have brains
in your head.
You have feet in
your shoes. You
can steer yourself
any direction you
choose. You're
on your own and
you know what you
know. And you
are the one who'll
decide where to go.

DR. SEUSS

EXPLORE every day.

Though the road
you're walking may
be well-traveled,
that does not
necessarily mean
it is leading to
your destination.

UNKNOWN

EXPLORE every day.

The reason for any
journey is this: in a
journey, discoveries
are made.

UNKNOWN

EXPLORE every day.

It doesn't matter
what road you
take, hill you
climb, or path
you're on, you
will always end
up in the same
place, learning.

RALPH STEVENSON

EXPLORE every day.

One small step
up the mountain
often widens your
horizon in all
directions.

E.H. GRIGGS

EXPLORE every day.

The road of life
can only reveal
itself as it is
traveled; each turn
in the road reveals
a surprise.

UNKNOWN

EXPLORE every day.

If the future road
looms ominous or
unpromising, and
the roads back
uninviting, then
we need to gather
our resolve and,
carrying only
the necessary
baggage, step
off that road into
another direction.

MAYA ANGELOU

EXPLORE every day.

We French found
it and called it
joie de vivre—
the joy of living.

RENEE REPOND

EXPLORE every day.

No matter how far
a person can go,
the horizon is still
way beyond you.

ZORA NEALE HURSTON

EXPLORE every day.

We leave behind
a bit of ourselves
wherever we've
been.

EDMOND HARACOURT

EXPLORE every day.

He who returns
from a journey
is not the same
as he who left.

EXPLORE every day.

May you always
find new roads
to travel; new
horizons to
explore; new
dreams to call
your own.

UNKNOWN

EXPLORE every day.